IRISH ADDRESS BOOK

ILLUSTRATED BY *Marian Clark*

CHRONICLE BOOKS
SAN FRANCISCO

First published in 1973 by
The Appletree Press Ltd
19–21 Alfred Street, Belfast BT2 8DL
Tel: + 44 232 243 074 Fax: + 44 232 246 756

Copyright © The Appletree Press Ltd, 1993

Printed in the EU. All rights reserved.
No part of this publication may be reproduced
or transmitted in any form or by any means,
electronic or mechanical, photocopying,
recording or in any information or retrieval
system, without permission in writing
from Chronicle Books.

A Little Irish Address Book

First published in the United States in 1994
by Chronicle Books, 275 Fifth Street,
San Francisco, CA 94103

ISBN: 0-8118-0765-7

9 8 7 6 5 4 3 2 1

A

A

✉

☎
☏
✉

☎
☏

A

✉	
📞	
☎	
✉	
📞	
☎	

B

✉
☎
☎
✉

☎
☎

B

✉

☎

✉

☎

B

✉

☎
☎
✉

☎
☎

C

✉

☎
☎
✉

☎
☎

C

C

✉
☎
☎
✉

☎
☎

D

✉

☎
☎

✉

☎
☎

D

✉
☎
☏
✉

☎
☏

E

✉

☎
☎
✉

☎
☎

E

F

✉

☎
☎
✉

☎
☎

F

G

✉

☎
☎
✉

☎
☎

G

H

H

✉
☎
☎
✉

☎
☎

I

✉
☎
☏
✉
☎
☏

I

✉

☎
☎
✉

☎
☎

J

J

✉
☎
☎
✉
☎
☎

K

K

✉

☎
☎
✉

☎
☎

L

✉

☎
☎
✉

☎
☎

L

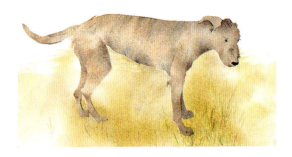

✉
☎
☎
✉
☎
☎

M

✉

☎

✉

☎

M

✉

☎
☎

✉

☎
☎

M

✉

☎
☎
✉

☎
☎

Mc

✉
☎
☎
✉

☎
☎

Mc

✉
☎
☎
✉

☎
☎

Mc

✉
☎
☏
✉
☎
☏

N

✉

☎
☎
✉

☎
☎

N

✉
☎
☎
✉

☎
☎

N

O

✉️

☎️
📠

✉️

☎️
📠

O

✉
☎
☎
✉
☎
☎

P

✉

☎
☎
✉

☎
☎

P

✉
☎
☎
✉

☎
☎

Q

✉

☎
☎
✉

☎
☎

Q

✉

☎
☎
✉

☎
☎

R

✉
☎
☏
✉

☎
☏

R

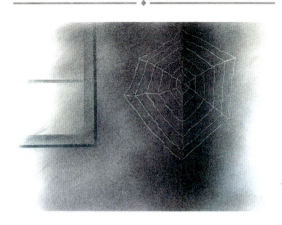

✉

☎
☎
✉

☎
☎

R

✉

☎
☏

✉

☎
☏

S

✉

☎
☎
✉

☎
☎

S

✉

☎
☎
✉

☎
☎

S

✉
☎
☎
✉
☎
☎

T

✉

☎
☎
✉

☎
☎

T

✉
☎
☎
✉
☎
☎

T

✉
☎
☏
✉
☎
☏

U

✉

☎
☎
✉

☎
☎

U

- ✉
- ☎
- ☎
- ✉
- ☎
- ☎

V

✉
☎
☎
✉

☎
☎

V

✉

☎
☎
✉

☎
☎

✉
☎
☎
✉

☎
☎

W

✉
☎
☎
✉
☎
☎

X

✉

☎
☎
✉

☎
☎

Y

✉

☎
☏
✉

☎
☏

Y

✉
_____
_____
_____

☎
☏
✉
_____
_____
_____

☎
☏

Z